IS
THERE
AN
ELEPHANT
IN MY
LIVING
ROOM?

Giuliano Sala Tenna

Ark House Press
PO Box 1722, Port Orchard, WA 98366 USA
PO Box 1321, Mona Vale NSW 1660 Australia
PO Box 318 334, West Harbour, Auckland 0661 New Zealand
arkhousepress.com

Cataloguing in Publication Data:
Title: Is There An Elephant In My Living Room
ISBN: 978-0-6489912-7-4 (pbk)
Subjects: Evangelism;

Design by initiateagency.com

ACKNOWLEDGEMENTS

F irstly, I would like to thank God, for his endur-
ing patience and grace throughout my life.
Despite my countless errors and wrongdoings,
he never shut the door on me or gave up on my
salvation.

I would also like to personally thank Warick
Smith and Allan Chapple for their encouragement
in writing this book along with their time in review-
ing the theological contents.

I would like to acknowledge my beautiful wife
who has been an incredible blessing in my life, an
encourager when I have felt down, a patient pseudo
editor who endured many proof readings, and my
best friend. Along with my two sons, you bring
incredible joy and happiness into my life.

Lastly, to my parents, siblings and close friends. I have been truly blessed to enjoy such great relationships and I only stand here today because of your contribution to my life.

I s there an elephant in my living room? No one seems to want to talk about it but I think they are just trying to be polite. Perhaps it's just easier if we all pretend it doesn't exist and enjoy the rest of the day. That seems to have worked well enough so far. If you disturb it then who knows what will happen, something that big and powerful, it could change your entire life. I think its name is Jesus.

Jesus.....

Jesus Who?

And why should you even care?

Jesus Christ, Muhammad, Buddha, Brahma. Aren't these all just central figures in different religions that humankind has manipulated and twisted over the centuries to control people and serve their own agenda? God or no God what difference does it make to you?

You're one person in a world with billions more just like you in a galaxy much bigger than most of us could possibly comprehend. Humankind has been debating the existence of God forever and neither side appears to be able to provide a definitive knockout blow. Or have they?

Ask yourself, how much time have you ever spent to really investigate the credibility of these central figures from any of these religions? What does history and archaeology have to say about Jesus? What about eye witnesses, science or millions of personal testimonies? How do we explain the fulfilment of pre-recorded prophecy or miracles?

If you are like me, then you have probably spent thousands of hours in your life working, exercising, studying, eating, sleeping, cleaning, travelling, playing and endless other activities, but for what? If you work an 8 hour day for 40 years of your life then you will spend more than 75,000 hours of your life at work! But for what purpose? To pay for "Stuff"! To be more successful? More desirable? To be more content and happy? What does happiness even look like to you? What does it even mean to be happy?

What if, when you started life there were two paths you could have walked down but you only ever saw the first path. You only ever saw the world with all its stuff and our physical bodies and you set off making the best of what you had. You worked in different ways all your life, busy setting and achieving the next goal, learning, growing, succeeding, doing. You never stopped to question if the path you were on was the right one or not. You were simply too busy for that, you just had to keep going hour after hour, day after day, year after year.

But what if there was a second path. One that no one ever told you about. A path that walks right alongside the path you are on only it is in the shade a little. It's a little less stressful, a little less noisy, a little less filled with stuff but somehow more satisfying. One that leads to an existence of some sort after this world is long gone.

Wouldn't you at least want to spend a few hours to investigate that path? If you're going to spend 75,000 hours of your life working to pay for stuff, don't you want to at least be sure that you are working for the right stuff?

The truth is most people never really stop and seriously investigate any of these historical figures. It's much easier to dismiss them all as fairy tales passed down from generation to generation which have slowly weaved their way into the fabric of our history but have little meaning to us today.

Surely an educated person in today's modern society cannot believe in a supernatural creator of the world. Surely science and archaeology alone can disprove this? But not so.

The truth is, to believe in God does require a position of faith as there are some things that cannot be explained fully with our current understanding of the scriptures. However, to NOT believe in God is also a position of faith as there are still many things that cannot be explained fully by science or modern thinking alone. If you choose not to believe in God, be aware that you still have a position of faith just as much as those who choose to believe in God. The person who does not believe in God, does not actually have all the answers. There are still many questions unanswered by science and all our intellectual thinking. It is still a position of faith as you simply believe there is not a God but there is some alternative that the world has not yet discovered to explain all the unanswered questions.

Please read that paragraph again, this is the single most important paragraph of this book and maybe even your life. **To believe or NOT to believe in God are both positions of faith**. To say "I don't believe" is not actually an answer to the question, what you should be asking yourself is what do you believe? Answering that question will answer for you which path in life you choose to walk. It is the single most important question for us all to answer in our lives as it is at the very core of who we are and how we live our lives.

If you think the direction of your life warrants at least a few hours of study and contemplation then continue to read on and see what the actual facts have to tell us about the life of Jesus Christ. Christianity after all stands or falls on the life, death and resurrection of Jesus Christ. Surely, if we can simply disprove some aspect of the Jesus narrative then we can just move on in our lives and put this entire religion thing to rest.

This book will focus on Jesus Christ, the New Testament in the Bible and the facts. I will leave opinion out of this discussion and just present you with the facts which are accepted across the mainstream of the secular and Christian world. There will always be extremists at both ends of the debate who provide extreme views as fact, **but they simply are not fact**. Usually a small amount of independent research will prove them to be false, so let's stay focused on what facts the consensus mainstream of the secular and religious worlds have to say about Jesus Christ and then it is up to you to decide on what you believe.

But please, let's not be lazy, don't be that person who gets to the end of their life and says" I just never really thought about it". To me that would be a tragic waste of a life. I'm sure you've tried many other things to find meaning or happiness so why not give this fairy tale of Jesus Christ a few hours of your time!

CHAPTER 1

A HISTORY LESSON

What do you think the world looked like 2,000 years ago when Jesus lived? Does that seem like a long time ago to you or not?

What is universally agreed across all historians is that humankind was operating in a civilised ordered society in the parts of the world which the narrative of Jesus Christ took place. The Roman Empire ruled over Jerusalem from 63 BC, they operated an ordered system involving Prefects who then distributed power to local administrators. Society was governed by laws and a court system. Commerce was transacted using barter or fiat currencies and there were commercial enterprises for industry from farming to construction. The cities and settlements had road systems, sewers, private ownership of land was recognised and they had class systems and professions. In many ways society was much like it is today just without the technological advances.

This is the first fact we need to accept. That humankind, at the time of Jesus Christ, was an ordered society that had the ability to accurately record historical events and preserve their integrity. It was not the age of the cave man or even the age of the nomad. Historical events were written and preserved in manuscripts, not left only to oral retellings which are more vulnerable to manipulation and embellishments.

If I were to guess, I would say you are familiar with the Greek philosopher and scientist Aristotle. He was born in the city of Stagira in Northern Greece around 384 BC and died around 322 BC (so he died over 300 years before the birth of Jesus Christ). At 17 or 18 years of age he joined Plato's Academy in Athens and remained there until age 37. He went on to tutor Alexander the Great at the beginning of 343 BC and he is largely regarded as one of the most influential thinkers of his time. He left us with such famous quotes like *"The whole is more than the sum of its parts"*, *"Happiness depends upon ourselves"* and *"It is the mark of an educated mind to be able to entertain a thought without accepting it"* along with many others.

No historian who is credible in his field doubts the existence and life of Aristotle. Yet surprisingly, we only have somewhere from 5 to 49 original manuscripts still in existence today which detail his life and works, the earliest of which are dated over 1,000 years after his death. Yet we do not question the authenticity of the life of Aristotle given the significant impact his teachings had on humankind for centuries to follow.

What about Julius Caesar? I'm sure you have all heard of him. Assassinated by his close friend Brutus with the support of the Roman Senate around 44 BC (similar time period to when Jesus was born). Julius Caesar had just been named perpetual dictator of the Senate in Rome and to this day you can stand at the very spot in Rome where historians believe his assassination occurred. Did you know that there are only 9 to 10 original manuscripts detailing the life and death of Julius Caesar which are still in existence today? The earliest one of these that we still have is dated 1,400 years after his death, yet we doubt not his existence.

There is a commonly employed technique used by historians where in order to validate a historical event they search for the ability to verify the event from as many manuscripts as possible from as many sources as possible to look for discrepancies. Have the stories been embellished over the centuries? Has mythology started to work its way into the story? They also place greater emphasis on works that can been traced back closer to the source of the events that are recorded such as eye witnesses and the like.

Considering the above example of Aristotle and Julius Caesar let's now turn to the New Testament and the life of Jesus Christ which is the focus of our study. The New Testament consists of 27 books which contain the 4 Gospels detailing the narrative of Jesus's life written by Matthew, Mark, Luke and John the Disciple. Matthew, Mark and John were all eye witnesses to many of the events recorded in the Gospels with each providing a different perspective. We will speak more about the importance of having different eye witness accounts in a later chapter. We then have 13 letters (books) written from Paul the Apostle to the early church across the region. Many of these early churches are in places which can still be visited today such as Corinth, Antioch and Ephesus and Paul's mission journeys can be physically retraced in detail. Paul was a convert to Christianity shortly after the death of Jesus and the earliest of his letters can be dated back to 49-65 AD so only 30 years or so after the death of Christ. There are then 4 additional books written by John the Disciple (an eye witness), 2 books written by Peter the Apostle & Disciple (another eye witness), a second book written by Luke and then single books written by James (an eye witness) and Jude with only the author of Hebrews uncertain.

So we have our source(s) named, many of whom were eye witnesses and we will establish their credibility as reliable eye witnesses later. The question right now is, have the stories been embellished over the centuries?

There are over 5,600 original manuscripts in Greek containing parts of the New Testament still in existence today. If you include other languages such as Latin then this balloons to over 24,000 manuscripts. Furthermore the earliest of the original manuscripts contained in the New Testament can be dated to somewhere from 49 to 65 years after the death of Jesus. Of the 24,000 copies named above there is a 99.5% accuracy in the translation of these from one language to another which is extraordinary from a historical perspective. This is a fact that is not in question. The New Testament and Jesus Christ's life has more original manuscripts and translations still in existence today than any other historical event of that era. Not by some small margin but by a large overwhelming volume.

What does this tell us about the life of Jesus Christ? It tells us that humankind believed the events that were happening were significant and warranted recording. That these events required the utmost care in translation and retelling of the narrative and that throughout history the preservation of these manuscripts was of more importance than any other as they were reproduced meticulously. It tells us that the people who were alive at the time of these events, truly believed something extraordinary had happened and that following generations had a strict system in place to ensure that the stories were not added to or subtracted from.

Perhaps this doesn't seem important to you, but I ask you to research another historical figure or event that is widely accepted by our society from say 1,000 BC until 1,000 AD. Perhaps the life of Marcus Aurelius, King Arthur or the fall of the Roman Empire. What you would find is that no other historical figure of that era has more original manuscripts or written "evidence", if you like, of his birth, life, death and teachings than Jesus Christ.

This in and of itself is not a reason to believe, but hopefully I am starting to prompt your interest that perhaps the New Testament is not a collection of nice fairy tales but rather historical documents that stand up to the toughest scrutiny. Furthermore, if they stand up to scrutiny as reliable historical documents, then you cannot have the view that the story of Jesus has been incorrectly reported, recorded or embellished but rather you must have a view that the events are either lies, a massive hoax of global proportions, or true. If you study other religious materials from other religions, they simply do not stand up to this level of scrutiny, that's a fact.

Let's turn our attention now and investigate what does secular history of this time have to say concerning Jesus Christ? Was it only in Christian circles that we have historical records detailing the life of Jesus?

The earliest non Christian writings of Jesus Christ was probably the Jewish historian Flavius Josephus who wrote the history of Judaism around 93 AD. He makes reference to "Jesus, the so called Christ". Remember the Jews as a race were not followers of Jesus, it was the Jewish religious teachers that plotted the death of Jesus as he was undermining their power base. So it is quite telling that a Jewish historian even bothers with mentioning Jesus. About 20 years after this we have the Roman politicians Pliny and Tacitus who held some of the highest offices at the beginning of the second century AD in the Roman Empire. From Tacitus we learn that Jesus was executed while Pontius Pilate was the Roman prefect in charge of Judaea (AD26-36) and Tiberius was emperor (AD14-37) – reports that fit with the timeframe of the gospels.

Pliny contributes the information that, where he was governor in northern Turkey, Christians worshipped Christ as a god. Neither of them liked Christians – Pliny writes of their "pig-headed obstinacy" and Tacitus calls their religion a destructive superstition. Strikingly, there was never any debate in the ancient world about whether Jesus of Nazareth was a historical figure. In the earliest literature of the Jewish Rabbis, Jesus was denounced as the illegitimate child of Mary and a sorcerer. Among pagans, the satirist Lucian and philosopher Celsus dismissed Jesus as a scoundrel, but we know of no one in the ancient world who questioned whether Jesus lived.

We have to always critically assess the information we are presented with. It is not the extremists to the left or the right that we should be listening to but rather the moderate in the middle. The consensus view is that there is no doubt that sometime around 5-6 BC to 30-36 AD there existed a man named Jesus Christ. He did things that couldn't be explained and he *claimed* to be the Son of God. He was executed under Pontius Pilate by crucifixion and following his death a great religious movement began, the followers of which were called Christians.

These are all FACTS. There is no opinion in these statements. No credible historian who has studied this era questions any of these statements. What Jesus claimed, that he is the Son of God, has been debated forever more but the facts concerning did he exist, at this time in history and did a religious movement start after his death are not in question at all.

Let that sit with you for a while. The New Testament is not regarded as a fairy tale in the academic world but rather historical texts. The question regarding did Jesus exist has been answered long ago in the affirmative. What he claimed is the matter of opinion, but his existence and historical records are without question. So if you previously thought Jesus may not have even been a real person, or the words in the New Testament had become twisted over the centuries, then both those considerations can now be dismissed as factually incorrect. Jesus is real and the New Testament is regarded as an accurate historical text. Fact.

CHAPTER 2

OFF TO THE SCIENCE LAB

L et's now turn our attention to what science has to say about the Bible and creation.

Most people who choose not to believe in the narrative of Jesus Christ and who have actually taken the time to research the subject, have scientific arguments at the cornerstone of their beliefs. Typically the two biggest items of discussion are concerned with the "Big Bang" theory versus creation by intellectual design, and then evolution of humankind from apes.

Let's begin with the "Big Bang" theory. The Big Bang theory proposes that under the right atmospheric conditions chemicals have an inherent ability to evolve into living cells. It theorizes that primitive earth was covered with pools of chemicals that provided with energy from lightning or the sun could be transformed into amino acids – which in theory are the building blocks of life – and then over billions of years evolution did the rest for these amino acids to evolve into animals and the like.

There was a landmark experiment hailed by supporters of this theory which was conducted by Stanley Miller at the University of Chicago. Miller recreated what he proposed was the atmospheric conditions of primitive earth in a laboratory and then shot electricity through it to simulate the effects of lightning. Before long, he found that amino acids had been created which provides the foundations for all life.

However, the assumptions for the experiment were fatally flawed from the outset. Miller had proposed that the atmosphere of primitive earth was composed of ammonia, methane and hydrogen which are the prerequisite components in physical chemistry to generate a suitable chemical reaction. Miller knew if you had chemicals like carbon dioxide or nitrogen then they wouldn't react.

Hence, Miller simply proposed the chemical composition for the atmosphere that he required to get the outcome he desired. The fact is that in the 1980s NASA scientists established that primitive earth never had any methane, ammonia or hydrogen in any quantity. Rather it was composed of water, carbon dioxide and nitrogen which is completely incompatible to generate the outcome Miller was seeking. Science, through extensive critical analysis, proved that while Miller's experiment was interesting, it simply did not present a valid theory for the creation of life. Miller in later life withdrew his proposed theory as a valid explanation for the origin of life.

For decades we were taught this theory in our schools as fact, but subsequent to this, modern science has proven it to be flawed!

There are obviously other scientific theories proposed regarding the origins of life. Some of them include random chance, chemical affinity, self ordering tendencies, vents in the ocean, life from outer space and so on. It is by no means my intention to try and address every one of these in this small book. However, I can state as fact, every one of these proposed theories has evaporated under scrutiny. At this present time, the consensus moderate thinking from science regarding the origins of life is simply at a dead end. Klaus Dose, a biochemist who is regarded as one of the foremost experts in the field commented "at present, all discussions on principal theories and experiments in the field either end in stalemate or in a confession of ignorance."

What about evolution? How do we reconcile evolution with the Biblical texts?

First of all we need to break down the theory of evolution into two sub-categories. There is evolution theories which refer to the changes in populations of organisms over time such as natural selection and genetic variations within the same species. This is referred to as micro evolution and is not in conflict with biblical texts. There is overwhelming evidence in support of micro evolution. Then there is the more extreme evolutionist theories that extrapolate out some assumptions over very long periods of time (millions of years) which they believe establish humankind has evolved from anthropoid apes (chimpanzees). This is in direct conflict with biblical texts which state humankind was created in the image of God.

Our study here will be limited to facts, not opinions, and will not attempt to prove creation. Rather it will simply prove that the theory concerning the evolution of humankind from apes is inherently flawed, even in the scientific world.

There is an enormous amount of research on this subject matter, overwhelming, but the key flaw in the evolution theory is the issue concerning the "missing link".

The Missing Link is concerned with the issue that throughout the entire study of archaeology, dating all the way back to the dinosaurs and beyond, there has been no fossils ever discovered that link humankind to apes. Evolutionists *believe* that there is some missing link dating 6 million to 10 million years ago that explains this transformation. The problem with this is archaeology has discovered thousands of fossils from the Mesozoic age to establish the existence of dinosaurs dating back 250 million years yet no fossils have ever been discovered linking humankind to apes even though the theorized time period for the ape-man is only 6 million to 10 million years ago. The ice age is believed to have occurred about 2.5 million years ago and the earth is currently believed to be circa 4.5 billion years old. Now there is much conjecture regarding this dating but remember we are focused on the consensus moderate view in society today not the extremists at either end. Focusing on the consensus view in science today it is generally accepted that radiometric dating methods using radioactive minerals that occur in rocks and fossils is the most accurate measure of the age of fossils. Based on the consensus scientific view of the age of the earth and dating of fossils we actually have a very large amount of evidence to support the existence of dinosaurs, which are much older than when the ape-man was proposed to have existed, yet we have no archaeological evidence linking humankind to apes.

It appears then science is not so much in conflict with the Biblical texts but rather science is in conflict with itself. You see, we have a situation where we have extensive archaeological evidence of over 700 different species of dinosaurs dating back 250 million years and yet the evolutionists are still looking for their missing link ape-man. A reasonable person would assume that if this ape-man was to survive the ice age that there must have been an abundance of ape-men roaming the earth at the time, so finding one fossil of such a thing would be probable. Yet we have found nothing. This is a fact. Evolutionists have no hard evidence that links the anthropoid apes to humankind, it is still a theory, it is often taught in our schools as fact but that is simply not true. **There has never been any archaeological proof of inter species evolution (human or otherwise) throughout our entire history**. Evolutionists simply refer to it as the "missing link" and seem to have no problem with this, or perhaps they simply choose to place their *faith* in this!

Let me demonstrate further how desperate the evolutionists are to find this missing link. In 1912 Charles Dawson, an amateur archaeologist claimed to have discovered the 'missing link' between ape and man. He had found part of a human-like skull in Pleistocene gravel beds near Piltdown village in Sussex, England. It has since been referred to as the Piltdown Man.

Dawson wrote to Arthur Smith Woodward, Keeper of Geology at the Natural History Museum at the time, about his find. Dawson and Smith Woodward started working together, making further discoveries in the area. They found a set of teeth, a jawbone, more skull fragments and primitive tools, which they suggested belonged to the same individual.

Smith Woodward made a reconstruction of the skull fragments, and the archaeologists *hypothesised* (ie theory not fact) that the find indicated evidence of a human ancestor living 500,000 years ago. They announced their discovery at a Geological Society meeting in 1912.

For the most part, their story was accepted in good faith. However, in 1949 new dating technology arrived that changed scientific opinion on the age of the remains using fluorine tests, Dr Kenneth Oakley, a geologist at the Natural History Museum, discovered that the Piltdown remains were only 50,000 years old. This eliminated the possibility of the Piltdown Man being the missing link between humans and apes as at this point in time humans had already developed into their *Homo sapiens* form.

Following this, biological anthropologist Dr Joseph Weiner and human anatomist Wilfrid Le Gros Clark, both from Oxford University, worked with Dr Oakley to further test the age of the Piltdown findings. Their results showed that the skull and jaw fragments actually came from two different species, a human and an ape, probably an orangutan. Scratches on the surfaces of the teeth, visible under the microscope, revealed that the teeth had been filed down to make them look human. They also discovered that most of the finds from the Piltdown site had been artificially stained to match the local gravels.

The conclusion (which is now universally accepted across the scientific world) is the Piltdown Man was an audacious fake and a sophisticated scientific fraud. Yet, at the time of the dis-

covery the mainstream of the evolutionist theo-
rists held up the Piltdown man as absolute proof
that humankind had descended from apes and that
the creation story was proven beyond doubt to be
false. For almost 40 years they believed they had
found the missing link and without detailed critical analysis they placed their *faith* in a fraud! How
devastating.

What does science really have to say about the
Biblical texts concerning creation? Not a lot. The
Big Bang theory has been proven to be flawed and
no current alternative theory is proposed by the science faculty while evolutionists are left with a missing link in their own theory. It seems to be that both
sides of this debate have positions of *faith* regarding
how humankind was created. While we have extensive factual information to detail the life of Jesus
Christ we do not have such evidence regarding the
Biblical creation of the earth so Christians have a

position of *faith* regarding the Biblical texts. But please, do not think that science has factual proof of the Big Bang or inter species evolution, that is simply wrong, both those theories require a position of *faith* just like the creationists. Science presents no definitive answers on this subject matter. Hence if you do not believe in God, or the accuracy of the Jesus narrative, on the basis of scientific evidence then you have been misled. Science does not provide a compelling argument for or against creation. Fact.

CHAPTER 3

LET'S STUDY SOME ROCKS

personally love the study of archaeology. Humankind has learned so much of our history from the thousands upon thousands of archaeological diggings conducted across our planet over hundreds of years. The careful recovery and analysis of material from all ages in our history continues to be one of the biggest sources of information to verify and expand on historical texts and our understanding of nature. From the dinosaurs through to events that happened in the last 100 years, we continue to learn more from archaeology about humankind and animal species than from perhaps any other discipline. Furthermore, as we saw in the previous chapter, archaeology also provided two of the key rebuttals to the "Big Bang" theory and inter-species evolution.

Let's now focus on what evidence, hard facts not opinions, that archaeology can provide to us regarding interpretation of certain biblical texts, as well as providing an independent way to check the Bible's historical reliability. Many critics of Christianity continue to argue against the trust-worthiness of the New Testament record but, in fact, every new archaeological find on the subject matter has been on the side of scripture, not the sceptics. To illustrate this let's consider just a hand-ful of examples. I apologise in advance as this will get a little technical in parts but it's important to understand that archaeology has provided us with specific technical proof of recorded events in the Bible.

Jerusalem and The Pool of Bethesda

In the gospel of John chapter 5 there is described a pool in Jerusalem, near the Sheep Gate, called Bethesda, surrounded by five covered colonnades. Until the 19th century, there was no evidence outside of John's gospel for the existence of this pool and John's unusual description caused Bible scholars to doubt the reliability. Remember, what we are looking for from the study of archaeology in relation to this matter is do we have factual evidence that confirms a specific event or place or accuracy of an author. If we do not, then the author or text may not be regarded as a reliable source of information. Furthermore if we have evidence the author is factually wrong, then credibility of the author's other writings could be brought into question.

After much scepticism for many centuries regarding the accuracy of John's writing on the subject matter, the pool was duly uncovered in the 1930s with four colonnades around its edges and one across its middle. Ian Wilson reports: "Exhaustive excavations by Israeli archaeologist Professor Joachim Jeremias have brought to light precisely such a building, still including two huge, deep-cut cisterns, in the environs of Jerusalem's Crusader Church of St Anne."

It appears John was in fact correct in the detail of his records adding credibility to his writings.

Jerusalem and The Pool of Siloam

Further in the gospel of John chapter 9 we read the story of Jesus healing a man who was born blind. Christ spits on the ground, makes some mud and puts it on the blind man's eyes. He then instructs the blind man to wash in the Pool of Siloam. The blind man does so, and is healed. Critics of scripture had for a long period of time assumed that John's Gospel contained fictional accounts of Christ's actions as there was no pool found where John claims Jesus was at this time. But after centuries of debate the existence of the Pool of Siloam was discovered in the exact location that John refers to in this text.

What had occurred was in the third century AD, a church was built above a pool attached to Hezekiah's water tunnel in Jerusalem to commemorate the healing of the blind man reported in John's Gospel. Until recently, this was thought to be the Pool of Siloam which was not in the correct location which John wrote about in his gospel. Critics argued that if John had got such a significant detail wrong then surely the credibility of the entire story is in question and the reliability of John as a source of information concerning these events is brought into question. However subsequent to this, during sewerage works in 2004, engineers stumbled upon the steps of a first century ritual pool near the mouth of Hezekiah's tunnel. By the summer of 2005, archaeologists said it was without doubt the missing Pool of Siloam and critics withdraw their scepticism regarding the accuracy of John's writing.

Nazareth

Despite its fame today in the phrase 'Jesus of Nazareth', the town where Jesus lived was so insignificant in biblical times that it isn't mentioned in any surviving literature until after the time of Jesus. Because of the lack of mention of Nazareth in the historical record, some critics have argued that the village didn't exist until after the time of Jesus and so Jesus couldn't have been from Nazareth, as it didn't exist until after his death.

Archaeology though says otherwise. The evidence on the ground in Nazareth gives a good indication of the ancient date of the village. For example, archaeological digs in the vicinity of Nazareth have discovered tombs dating from the first century AD confirming the village was a strongly Jewish settlement. Then, in December 2009, archaeologists from the Israeli Antiquities Authority, excavating in the grounds of a former convent, unearthed a house from first century Nazareth. According to excavation director Yardenna Alexandre: "The discovery is of the utmost importance since it reveals for the very first time a house from the Jewish village of Nazareth and thereby sheds light on the way of life at the time of Jesus." It also provided clear evidence of Nazareth definitely being the site of a village before Jesus birth.

Peter's (the Apostle and Disciple of Jesus) house in Capernaum

Capernaum contains the remains of a church from the fifth century AD which is octagonal in shape. In 1968, archaeologists discovered the remains of an earlier church underneath it. This had been built around what was originally a private house, which was apparently used by Christians as a meeting-place during the second half of the first century. Today a modern church exists, suspended above the site, with the excavation site visible through a glass floor.

Peter Walker, professor of Biblical Studies at Trinity School for Ministry, says: "Graffiti that referred to Jesus as Lord and Messiah provides strong evidence that the room was used as a place of Christian worship – almost certainly because it was believed to be the room used by Jesus, perhaps the home of Simon Peter (Luke 4:38). Given that the early tradition goes back to the first century, this is almost certainly the very place where Jesus stayed – the home of his chief apostle, Peter."

The Pontius Pilate stone

In 1961, an inscription was found which confirms not only the rule of Pilate in Judea but also his preference for the title 'Prefect'.

The 'James, son of Joseph, brother of Jesus' ossuary

James the brother of Jesus was martyred in AD 62. A mid first century AD chalk ossuary (tomb) discovered in 2002 bears this inscription: "James, son of Joseph, brother of Jesus" *("Ya'akov bar Yosef akhui di Yeshua")*

The ossuary has provoked controversy as the inscription was originally suspected of being a forgery. However, two eminent paleographers confirmed the authenticity in 2012. New Testament scholar Ben Witherington states: "If, as seems probable, the ossuary found in the vicinity of Jerusalem and dated to about AD 63 is indeed the burial box of James, the brother of Jesus, this inscription is the most important extra-biblical evidence of its kind."

Evidence of Crucifixions

In 1968 an ancient burial site was uncovered containing about 35 bodies. One named Yohanan Ben Ha'galgol had a 7 inch nail driven through both feet. Yohanan's legs were crushed by a blow consistent with the common use of Roman 'crucifragium' proving that this method of punishment was used during Jesus' time.

Leprosy in the First Century

Some have suggested that there was no 'leprosy' (i.e. *Mycobacterium Leprae* or Hansen's Disease) in the Middle East in Jesus's day and hence the healing of the lepers must have been fabricated. However, thanks to archaeology there is now dramatic evidence of its existence in the early first century. Scientific testing of the burial shroud in the so-called 'Shroud Tomb' has confirmed the presence of lepros. Accelerator Mass Spectrometry (AMS) radio carbon dating confirmed the first-century date of both shroud and skeletal remains. DNA testing confirmed that the man wrapped in the shroud was related to other members whose skeletal remains were recovered in the tomb. This DNA testing also revealed that the man had suffered from leprosy.

Bethlehem

In May 2012 the Israel Antiquities Authority announced the discovery of a bulla (a small clay seal) that mentions Bethlehem, the birthplace of Jesus. A bulla is a piece of clay that was used for sealing a document or object. The bulla was impressed with the seal of the person who sent the document or object, and its integrity was evidence the document or object was not opened by anyone unauthorized to do so. Three lines of ancient Hebrew script appear on the bulla:

Bishv'at
BatLechem
[Lemel]ekh

According to Eli Shukron, director of the excavation on behalf of the Israel Antiquities Authority,

'it seems that in the seventh year of the reign of
a king (it is unclear if the king referred to here is
Hezekiah, Manasseh or Josiah), a shipment was dis-
patched from Bethlehem to the king in Jerusalem.'
Shukron emphasizes, 'this is the first time the name
Bethlehem appears outside the Bible, in an inscription from the First Temple period, which proves
that Bethlehem was indeed a city in the Kingdom
of Judah, and possibly also in an earlier period.'

The Synagogue in Capernaum

Jesus taught in the synagogue in Capernaum
according to Mark 1:21-22 and Luke 4:31-36.
Luke 7:1-10 records how Jesus healed the slave
of a Roman centurion posted locally. The people
encouraged Jesus to heal the slave because the
Roman officer had built their synagogue. The black
basalt foundations of this 1st century synagogue

(a dating confirmed by pottery finds beneath the floor) can be seen today under the remains of the 4th century lime-stone synagogue in Capernaum.

Herod the Great

Confirmation of Herod the Great from a bronze coin. On the bottom side there is a tripod and ceremonial bowl with the inscription 'Herod king' and the year the coin was struck, 'year 3' (of Herod's reign), or 37 BC.

Furthermore, in 1996 Israeli Professor of Archaeology Ehud Netzer discovered in Masada a piece of broken pottery with an inscription, called an ostracon. This piece had Herod's name on it and was part of an amphora used for transportation (probably wine), dated to c. 19 BC. The inscription is in Latin and reads, *"Herod the Great King of the Jews (or Judea)"*, the first such that mentions the full title of King Herod.

To summarise, critics sometimes argue there's no hard evidence for the New Testament narrative, but archaeology says otherwise. Archaeology gives us independent evidence for cultural practices, beliefs, places and people mentioned in the New Testament. This evidence confirms the historical character and reliability of the New Testament texts. This is by no means an exhaustive list, there are entire books dedicated to the subject matter so please investigate further if this is something that resonates with you. What we can conclude, factually, is that **no archaeological discovery has ever controverted a biblical reference** and scores of archaeological findings have been made which confirm in detail historical statements in the Bible.

Archaeology does not confirm 100% of the events in the Bible, nor would we expect it to.

However, there has never in the history of the study been a substantiated archaeological discovery that has contradicted any of the references in the Bible. This is absolutely extraordinary for a document which contains texts written almost 2,000 years ago. One of the critical questions to ask is "if the Bible and New Testament stories were fabricated then why are the authors so specific regarding the dates and places of events occurring?" Think about this, when we lie, we generally try to keep the facts "general" so we don't get caught out in the detail. If the Biblical stories were all part of some incredible hoax spanning generations, then wouldn't the writers try to keep the stories general, not name specific places and dates. This is what we actually do see with some of the other world religions. They keep the stories high level and more philosophical, miracles are performed in private not public (no eye witnesses), exact places of events are not named so future generations cannot verify them. But this is not the case with the New Testament. It is very specific on many occasions. It is actually challenging the reader to say "if you want proof, go to this place, you will find what I speak of".

Archaeology provides overwhelming proof that the New Testament is an accurate historical document with the highest level of integrity regarding the record of events. While archaeology cannot confirm all of the events in the New Testament, it does provide us with evidence time and time again regarding the historical accuracy of the New Testament text. Furthermore, the critical conclusion is that not on one occasion does anything from the study of archaeology contradict anything in the New Testament. Basically, there is evidence from the study of archaeology that supports the New Testament texts and nothing from archaeology that disproves or discredits it. Fact.

CHAPTER 4

ORDER PLEASE, THIS COURT IS NOW IN SESSION

I n modern society when we have disagreements, more times than not, it ends up being settled in a court of law. The evidence is presented to a judge or jury, arguments are made, witnesses are questioned, documents are submitted and theories are provided.

In a civil law matter the standard of proof is "it is more probable than not that what the person says happened is true." In criminal law matters the standard is "proof beyond reasonable doubt", so a slight variance but similar.

When considering the standard of poof there are four general types of evidence that can be provided:

- Real evidence (tangible things, such as a weapon)
- Demonstrative (a model of what likely happened at a given time and place)
- Documentary (a letter, blog post, or other document)
- Testimonial (eye witness testimony)

Bearing this in mind, let's now apply these tests to the New Testament and the narrative of Jesus.

We have already covered the first three points in previous sections. We have archaeology which has provided us with real evidence such as tangible artefacts from the time of Jesus confirming places where some events in the New Testament took place. Furthermore we have no real evidence from archaeology or any other tangible evidence that contradicts anything contained in the New Testament. We are presented with a demonstrative model of what likely was proposed to have happened (via the gospels) at various times and places and this is supported in part by real evidence. We have extensive documentary evidence via the volume of original texts and manuscripts that have been preserved through the ages in Christian and secular societies. So really, we need to focus in this chapter on the testimonial evidence and the credibility of the witnesses as eye witness testimony is given great weight in a court of law.

Notice I said testimonial evidence and the **credibility** of the witnesses. This is a critical point. People can lie. No surprise there. In a court of law it is about credible witnesses, is the person presenting the evidence of good character? Do they have ulterior motives? Could they simply have got the events wrong due to their point of view? These are the sorts of questions we should be asking ourselves concerning the testimonial evidence for or against the Jesus narrative.

The testimonial evidence for or against Jesus's birth, life and death is focused on the four gospels contained in the New Testament. The four gospels are four books in the Bible that retell the same story from four different perspectives being Matthew, Mark, Luke and John. Who are these people? Matthew was a tax collector who became one of Jesus's twelve disciples. Mark was the son of a Jerusalem widow whose home was a meeting place for the early believers. Mark recorded the events as he heard them firsthand from the disciple Peter. Luke was a companion of Paul the apostle and was a gentile (ie not from Jewish heritage) and a medical doctor while John was also one of the original twelve disciples. I know this may be confusing but stay with me, basically we have four witnesses in our case who have provided demonstrative and documentary evidence and we now have to critically assess their version of events.

To do this, we can consider a number of tests commonly used in a court of law. First of all we should consider the character test which looks at whether it was in the character of the witnesses to be truthful. Was there any evidence of dishonesty or immorality that might taint their testimony? Did the writers change their testimony under pressure, under threats of physical harm? Was their testimony consistent over time?

We know that Mark died a gruesome death when he returned to Alexandria as the people there rebuked his teachings against the pagan Gods. It is recorded they put a rope around his neck and dragged him through the streets until he was dead. Luke was believed to have been hung from an Olive Tree for his ministry works. Matthew was crucified in Turkey and only John died of natural causes in Ephesus around 98 AD. Despite the intense persecution placed on these eye witnesses there is no recorded evidence of even one of them recanting on a single detail that was written in the four gospels. Translate that to modern day terms, it means that even though all endured imprisonment or threats, physical violence and gruesome deaths, not one of them ever changed their stories. This is an incredible testament in itself of the character of our eye witnesses. You would think if any of them were lying or embellishing the story then under this sort of intense pressure at least one would break. But this is not the case. Why is that? Is it because they were so committed to all corroborating with one another to maintain the hoax, even under threat of death, or was it simply because it was the truth and hence they would rather die telling the truth then to lie and have their life spared. Regardless, it speaks volumes to their individual character.

Next we need to consider ulterior motives. When people testify, it's common that they might try to protect themselves or others by conveniently leaving out details that might be embarrassing. Rather than lie, they might simply just not tell the entire story. This is not what we find though when we read the four gospels. What we find is actually the opposite of this, we find all kinds of embarrassing details recorded by our eye witnesses. For example, the writers highlight different flaws in their character, that on many occasions they had little faith, that they didn't understand who Jesus was until he was gone, that Peter denied Jesus three times upon his arrest, that most of them abandoned

Jesus after his death and so on. It doesn't appear they tried to paint themselves in an overly good light or make it out that they had it right all along.

What other ulterior motives could they have had? Perhaps they were trying to gain fame, fortune or women? Perhaps it was power or social standing? But let's think through this. Their testimonies turned their own cultural systems upside down teaching that people could come directly to God, you didn't need to go to the religious teachers or even them, so they were not creating a new power base for them to control. Their testimonies proposed a slave and a master are of the same value in God's kingdom even though none of them were slaves, so they personally gained nothing from this. They proposed that the first would be last and the last first. They were very confronting testimonies and led to them all being isolated in the Jewish society. They were no longer welcomed in the

Synagogues, which were at the heart of the Jewish culture. They were rejected by both the Gentiles (non Jewish population) and the Jews. There appears no ulterior motive for their testimonies. They gained nothing financially, they gained no social standing or political power, no fame or fortune for their works. They simply provided their account of the events with no personal gain.

Could they then, perhaps just have got it wrong? Were they so caught up in the moment that they all started feeding off each other's stories and lost track of the facts? Were there other people present who would have spoken up if the gospels had distorted the facts? An adverse witness? After all there were many people present from the Romans to the Jewish religious teachers who wanted to discredit Jesus as just another crazy man. Yet we have nothing in any subsequent historical records, which is widely accepted across the mainstream, which contradicts or proposes that the gospels were not accurate records of the events. We have no one arguing any of the key points, that Jesus was born around 5-6 BC in Bethlehem, that he was raised by Joseph and Mary, that around the age of 30 he started preaching and doing things that couldn't be explained (miracles), that he was arrested by the Romans in collaboration with the Jewish religious leaders, was handed over to Pontius Pilate, crucified, buried and then three days later his tomb was empty and people claim to have seen a resurrected Jesus. None of this is contested in any widely accepted subsequent historical documents.

You have to stop and reflect on this. If the above events were a hoax then people would have spoken up at the time. You can maybe get a few thousand people to agree on a scam but not an entire population. It's not actually **reasonable** to believe that an entire population, across different ethnic groups and classes were all in on some big hoax. That's absurd. If there were lies being told then at least some people in the broader population would have brought attention to this in a credible manner, with facts, but there is no record of anything of this nature occurring.

What we have here, are four independent witnesses who have provided their accounts of the events. They appear of good character and have no ulterior motives to embellish their testimony. There are no adverse witnesses who are arguing against what they have proposed and we have tangible evidence (artefacts) and documentary evidence (manuscripts) to support their testimonies.

Your honour, I find the standard of proof met!

CHAPTER 5

THE GREATEST FULFILMENT OF PRE-RECORDED PROPHECY IN THE HISTORY OF THE WORLD!

What is a prophecy? Put simply, a prophecy is a prediction of something that will happen in the future. To be credible it must have been recorded somewhere, usually in text, prior to the event occurring and the integrity of that record is not in question. If multiple sources of the recorded prophecy can be established then obviously there is more credibility that the prophecy was true.

The record keeping and historical integrity of the prophecy is of the utmost importance to have confidence that someone did not simply come along after the event, record it, and then propose that it was a prophecy written before the event occurred.

What does prophecy have to do with the factual evidence to support the Jesus narrative?

To understand this we first need to take a step back and understand what the Bible consists of. This is going to get a little bit into religion but please stay with me as we will keep it grounded in facts.

The Bible is basically a collection of many "books" and this collection is divided into two main time periods. The first being the Old Testament which is everything that happened before the birth of Jesus and then the second being the New Testament which contains everything from the birth of Jesus through to his death and then the early works of the apostles as the Christian faith spread. There are 39 books in the Old Testament and 27 in the New Testament.

In our study so far, we have been focused on the New Testament. However, in this section we are going to study what the Old Testament books tell us, predict if you like, about the coming Messiah (Jesus?).

A bit of background on the Old Testament. The Old Testament is also referred to as the Hebrew Bible or Tanakh and it is a collection of writings first compiled and preserved as the sacred books of the Jewish people. It is the most important collection of religious scriptures in the Jewish faith and the texts were written between 1,500 BC to 400 BC (Not that old when you consider the ice age was 2.5 million years ago). While the arrangement and numbering of the books in the Old Testament is different to the Tanakh, without getting into a deep theological discussion, the contents of the two are the same. Contained in both are a collection of books from the twelve minor Prophets Hosea, Joel, Amos, Obadiah, Jonah, Micah, Nahum, Habakkuk, Zephaniah, Haggai, Zechariah and Malachi and then the four major prophets Isaiah, Jeremiah, Ezekiel and Daniel. These prophets spoke prophetic words many of which concern signs for the coming Messiah. I said at the beginning of this book that I would focus on facts not opinion so let me do just that.

Prophecy in relation to Jesus Christ is the pre-recorded word of prophets from the Old Testament, or Tanakh, that was then fulfilled through his birth, life and death. The record keeping of these prophecies is in no doubt as they were meticulously recorded and preserved in the Jewish faith through the centuries. This means these prophecies could not be tampered with after the event to make the prophecy fit the events. You must remember the Jewish religious teachers were the main opponents of Jesus Christ. It was the Jewish religious teachers of the time that had Jesus arrested and insisted on his crucifixion as they believed he was committing blasphemy by claiming to be the Son of God. I appreciate this is probably getting a bit too "religious" for you, but the fact which we need to establish here is important. It is that there is absolutely no motivation or hidden benefits for the Jewish religious teachers to somehow, after the death of Jesus, then go back and change the prophecies contained in the Tanakh to fit the Jesus narrative. The keepers of the Jewish religion at the time were effectively the people who conspired to have Jesus killed, all through history the Jewish authorities have forcefully denied that Jesus was a prophet from God, let alone the Messiah spoken about in the Old Testament. So why would they have amended their religious books to make it appear he fulfilled ancient prophecies? They wouldn't. Furthermore, the Jewish faith and teachings was already very well established before the birth of Jesus and well known by the people, so if anyone tried to retrospectively change anything contained in the Tanakh, it would have met with strong opposition and never been permitted by the broader Jewish community. But we see no evidence of this in any historical records. By focusing on the prophecies contained in the Tanakh it gives us a reliable unbiased non Christian source of prophecy, which was recorded in text, with many copies in circulation at the time and subject to critical assessment.

Therefore, we can conclude that the prophecies contained in the Old Testament / Tanakh are the same today as when they were originally recorded and that the integrity of these prophecies are not questioned in either the secular or religious world. That is a fact.

It is generally accepted the New Testament record of the Jesus narrative fulfils 200 to 400 of the prophecies that were contained in the Old Testament / Tanakh. These prophecies are specific enough that the mathematical probability of Jesus fulfilling even a handful of them, let alone all of them, is staggeringly improbable, if not impossible. Once again, there are entire books dedicated to this subject matter so if this resonates with you then please research this more.

While fulfilment of many of the prophecies are open to interpretation, there are 55 fulfilled prophecies which have detailed evidence to support them. I'm very mindful, you want facts not religious opinions, so let's get some examples which are specific in their detail and where we have factual proof to support their fulfilment. I will provide the prophecy, the source in the Old Testament / Tanakh and then an explanation as to how this was fulfilled.

The Christ will be born in Bethlehem

Prophecy:

"But you, Bethlehem Ephrathah, though you are small among the clans of Judah, out of you will come for me one who will be ruler over Israel, whose origins are from of old, from ancient times." (Micah 5:2).

Fulfilment:

Bethlehem Ephrathah was a small town near Jerusalem on the West Bank of the Jordan River. It was the home town of King David who is an important character in the Old Testament / Tanakh. It is important to trace the genealogy from Abraham to David and then David to Jesus as the

Messiah was to come from the line of David and David was from Bethlehem. The genealogy (family tree) of Jesus can be traced back as follows, generation by generation:

1. Abraham
2. Isaac
3. Jacob
4. Judah and *Tamar*
5. Perez
6. Hezron
7. Ram
8. Amminadab
9. Nahshon
10. Salmon and *Rachab*
11. Boaz and *Ruth*
12. Obed
13. Jesse
14. David and *Bathsheba*
15. Solomon
16. Rehoboam
17. Abijah
18. Asa
19. Jehoshaphat
20. Jehoram
21. Uzziah
22. Jotham
23. Ahaz
24. Hezekiah
25. Manasseh
26. Amon
27. Josiah
28. Jeconiah

29. Shealtiel	36. Eliud
30. Zerubbabel	37. Eleazar
31. Abiud	38. Matthan
32. Eliakim	39. Jacob
33. Azor	40. Joseph
34. Zadok	41. Jesus
35. Achim	

This is very important as we have secular evidence that The Census of Quirinius was a census of Judea taken by Publius Sulpicius Quirinius, Roman governor of Syria, upon the imposition of direct Roman rule in Judea in 6 BC, the proposed time that Jesus was born.

As part of the census, everyone was required to return to their home town on their father's side to be counted in the census.

Therefore we have evidence that Joseph, who was of the line of David, returned to Bethlehem in the year 6 BC (the year of Jesus's birth) for the census taken by Publius Sulpicius Quirinius. We have a place named in prophecy for the birth of the Messiah and then we have evidence placing Jesus in that place at the specific time that a census was called.

Please note, Bethlehem was a very small fairly insignificant town. The fact that prophecy named such a small town for the Messiah to come from is an example of specific detail given in prophecy that was fulfilled by Jesus.

The nations will be blessed through Jacob's offspring

Prophecy:

"Your descendants (speaking of Jacob) will be like the dust of the earth, and you will spread out to the west and to the east, to the north and to the south. All peoples on earth will be blessed through you and your offspring" (Genesis 28:14).

Fulfilment:

Jacob is part of Jesus' genealogy as you can see from the family tree in our previous discussion. This is very interesting as it's not something that could be faked. If Jesus claimed to be of Jacob's and David's lineage but he was not, then people at the time would say "why do you say these things, we know Joseph (your father) and he is not of this line". But again, despite the fact that all this was written and circulated after Jesus's death, no one contested these facts. If they were untrue then they would have been contested. The Jewish religious leaders in particular who wanted to discredit Jesus's claims, would have contested that this was a lie. But instead we have silence from them, suggesting the written genealogy is correct.

Christ's ministry would begin in Galilee

Prophecy:

"Nevertheless, there will be no more gloom for those who were in distress. In the past he humbled the land of Zebulun and the land of Naphtali, but in the future he will honour Galilee of the nations, by the Way of the Sea, beyond the Jordan— The people walking in darkness have seen a great light; on those living in the land of deep darkness a light has dawned" (Isaiah 9:1–2).

Fulfilment:

In the four gospels, which we have previously established are reliable historical texts, the ministry of Jesus begins with his baptism in the countryside of Roman Judea and Transjordan, near the river Jordan, and ends in Jerusalem. The Gospel of Luke (Luke 3:23) states that Jesus was "about 30 years of age" at the start of his ministry. A chronology of Jesus typically has the date of the start of his ministry estimated at around AD 27–29 and the end in the range AD 30–36.

Jesus' early Galilean ministry begins when after his baptism, he goes back to Galilee from his time in the Judean desert. In this early period he preaches around Galilee and recruits his first disciples who begin to travel with him and eventually form the core of the early Church. The major Galilean ministry which begins in Matthew 8 includes the commissioning of the Twelve Apostles, and covers most of the ministry of Jesus in Galilee. The final Galilean ministry begins after the death of John the Baptist as Jesus prepares to go to Jerusalem.

Jesus would teach in parables

Prophecy:

"My people, hear my teaching; listen to the words of my mouth. I will open my mouth with a parable; I will utter hidden things, things from of old" (Psalm 78:1–2)

Fulfilment:

A parable is a simple story used to illustrate a moral or spiritual lesson. There are 46 parables contained in the four gospels of the New Testament which are spoken words from Jesus. There is no historical evidence which disputes the origin of the parables being Jesus.

He will be betrayed for 30 pieces of silver

Prophecy:

"I told them, 'If you think it best, give me my pay; but if not, keep it.' So they paid me thirty pieces of silver. "And the Lord said to me, 'Throw it to the potter'—the handsome price at which they valued me! So I took the thirty pieces of silver and threw them to the potter at the house of the Lord" (Zechariah 11:12–13).

Fulfilment:

This was fulfilled when Judas Iscariot betrayed Jesus into the hands of the Roman guards. It is documented in each of the four gospels. Furthermore the detail is quite specific in the prophecy as it names the amount "30 pieces" and it names the type of coin "silver" not gold or copper. Not bad for a prediction made 600 years before the event.

They would pierce Christ's hands and feet

Prophecy:

"Dogs surround me, a pack of villains encircles me; they pierce my hands and my feet" (Psalm 22:16).

And

"He protects all of his bones, not one of them will be broken:
(Psalm 34:20)

Fulfilment:

In John 19:36-37 it states 'Not one of his bones will be broken,' and 'they will look on the one they have pierced'". Furthermore Luke 23:39-41 we are told he was crucified and hung between two criminals (villains) "One of the criminals who hung there hurled insults at him: 'Aren't you the

Christ? Save yourself and us!' But the other criminal rebuked him".

What does this all mean? The sceptic would argue that Jesus knew some of these prophecies and therefore endeavoured to fulfil them. He could have chosen to minister in Galilee and speak in parables to get people thinking he was the Messiah. But then how do you explain that he was born in the correct lineage in the exact right town? How does someone fake this when people at the time could call that out to be a lie if it were not true? What about his betrayal? How did he instruct the Jewish Leaders to pay the specific amount of money in the prophecy for his betrayal when they were trying to discredit him? How did he control what happened to him on the cross to ensure no bones were broken. It was standard practice for the Roman guards to break the prisoner's legs at the end of a crucifixion to ensure they were dead before they were taken off the cross. This is well documented in secular historical records yet in Jesus's case they pierced his side. Did Jesus have a side deal going on with the Roman centurions while he hung dying on the cross? Highly unlikely.

Remember, we have only touched on 6 prophecies that were fulfilled. At a minimum there is universally agreed to be 55 prophecies that were fulfilled by Jesus life, ministry, death and resurrection. At the high end it is suggested there is up to 400 prophecies that were fulfilled although some of these are open to interpretation of the scriptures. Do you know what the probability of a single person fulfilling 55 prophecies written 1,500 to 400 years before he is born? It's basically impossible. The probability of one person fulfilling even 8 of the prophecies is so low that it is not measurable.

I hear sceptics say "If God was real, wouldn't he give us more proof?" I simply respond that we have somewhere up to 400 pieces of proof given to us in the Old Testament regarding who the Messiah would be. God did not want us to be tricked by some charlatan. We were given a large number of prophecies to confirm the identity of the person when the Messiah arrived. It was not left to chance as the mathematical probability of someone accidentally fulfilling this many prophecies is not possible. Nor was it left to a small elite group to decide who the Messiah was, as we see in other religions. No, we were given a long list of prophecies to look for to ensure the identity of the Messiah was beyond any doubt, you just have to look and the proof is right in front of you.

CHAPTER 6

MILLIONS OF LIVES

Throughout this book, I've presented you with a lot of facts supported by hard evidence. I now want to change up the pace and consider the personal evidence we have all around us, in every country across this world, spoken in every language, by all races and ethnic groups.

That is the evidence concerning millions upon millions of lives which have been personally impacted by the Jesus narrative.

Consider this, if someone you had never previously met tells you a nice story about a place you should visit on your next holiday, you might not think much of it. How do they know you will enjoy it as they did? You don't know this person, they don't know you so how could they know what you like on holidays, what holidays have they even been on anyway? Maybe they haven't seen as much of the world as you so they are just easily impressed. In any case, it would be unlikely to leave a lasting impression upon you and you would be unlikely to investigate this place any further.

Let's say sometime later you meet another person who is a distant associate of yours and they tell you the same story about this place. There are many similarities with the story the first person told you but some bits are different as their personal experience of this place is inevitably different. You ask your associate if they knew of the first person you met and they say "no, I've never heard of them". After this second encounter maybe you think "that's interesting" but you still probably wouldn't really take much notice of it.

Let's say you start travelling a lot for work and you are travelling to countries all over the world, you meet people from all different cultures, some speak different languages, some have had an easy life, some a hard life, some are successful people, some are not, some have terrible illnesses, some have great fame and fortune and some are very poor and.... they all keep telling you the same story about this great place you should visit! They all speak as if nothing else really matters, they tell you that you just have to go to this place and see it for yourself, and it will change your life. Would it not start to make you think "I really need to go see this place for myself, all these people can't just be making it up?"

Sure there will be some differences in the stories, if there were not you would actually become suspicious and think it was a hoax. Their stories are different because they are each person's individual experience of this place. Some of the people are acting a bit crazy and some of them aren't really the "type" of people you would normally hang out with, but some of them are actually pretty similar to you. You're pretty certain that there is no possibility that all these people you have met know each other as they are from all over the world and many of them don't even speak the same language. What's even more amazing is that the poor people you met have been to the same place as the wealthy people and they have had some similarities in their stories. The healthy people were telling stories that were similar to what the sick people had also been telling you. The person you met in Africa and the other person you met in Asia also spoke about some things in common. What is going on here? Could this place be real?

This is exactly what is happening to this very day with regards to Jesus Christ. There are people from every country, every race and ethnic background, rich and poor, healthy and sick, ordinary people and famous ones, all speaking different languages with different cultural backgrounds and yet they are all having similar personal experiences with Jesus Christ.

There are recorded instances where a person, who has been born in a remote village, from a cultural background that is not supportive of the Christian faith, in some extreme cases even where they have never seen a Bible, that testify to knowing Jesus Christ with similarities in their experiences to other people who are educated theologians.

The fact is this has happened, on many occasions, and is without question still happening to this day. You can argue about what they testify to, but you cannot argue that this is not occurring. Sceptics will say, these people are in such desperate personal circumstances that they have a psychological episode where they create this experience with Jesus as a coping mechanism. But some of these people didn't even know the name Jesus or the concepts in the Bible before their experiences. Some of these people have come from strict alternative religious cultures where they have been taught nothing of Jesus. What happens in these people's lives that they would turn their back on their family, friends and entire cultural environment to proclaim such a lie?

Why is it that throughout history we see that where the Christian faith is the most persecuted, the growth in believers is the greatest? Take for example China, where Christianity was brutally persecuted during the cultural revolution of 1966 – 1976. What followed was the fastest growing Christian population of anywhere in the world which has increased one hundred fold since the darkest days. What about in North Korea today?

Christians can be executed or sent for life imprisonment simply for not recanting their faith yet somehow people continue to tell of their personal experiences with Christ and somehow the Christian faith has endured.

I understand the psychology of people "wanting" to believe in something better. But I'm not talking about a small sample size though. We are talking about millions upon millions of people. The statistical probability that somehow people across all cultures and history are feeding off each other's stories is simply not possible.

Think about it, our sample size is large, we have a long observation period (at least 2,000 years), it is across all demographics, cultures, languages and age groups. It includes people who are successful, depressed, strong willed, educated, illiterate, dying, powerful and everything else in between. It is probably the biggest and longest sample size ever in the history of humankind, and it keeps repeating the same story over and over again.

Does it not make you think?

Some scams can last years, they can expand across countries and language barriers, they can fool some smart people but eventually they all fall down. Yet we now have 2,000 years of stories, personal stories from millions of people telling us about their personal experiences with God. It is not reasonable to consider that this is some elaborate scam that has somehow withstood 2,000 years of critical assessment.

Ultimately, this is the final and most compelling piece of evidence you can ever have. To have your own personal experience when the penny drops and you realise Jesus Christ was actually a real person and God is real. Suddenly, all the pieces of the puzzle fit together and you start to see the world through totally different eyes.

This week, just try saying to yourself "God is real". Wake up in the morning and just say quietly to yourself "God is real". **Just consider the possibility that statement is the truth** and not a lie. Just consider it.

What does that change in your life?

EVERYTHING!

CHAPTER 7

THE END IS REALLY JUST THE BEGINNING

This book was never intended to be a thorough study regarding the questions of life. It was not intended to provide you with all the answers or address in depth the detailed responses to each of the arguments that sceptics will raise against there being a God.

There are literally thousands and thousands of books and articles written for and against the subject matter and in this fast paced world it's hard enough to find a couple of spare hours in your week let alone the years required to thoroughly investigate all the material. This book was only intended to be like a small life raft bobbing in the ocean.

We are all trying our best to navigate this massive ocean we call "life". The vast majority of us just simply want to be loved and to love. To improve our lot a little, enjoy our family and friends and have a few nice things. But slowly life throws stuff at us, hard stuff. Some stuff hurts really bad and it changes us. Some stuff we will struggle with all our lives. Sometimes other people do awful things to us beyond what we can comprehend. There are all sorts of wars, violent crimes and terrible injustices and we start to think there is just no way there can be a loving God that created it all.

Then we start to listen to what the world has to say. "There's no proof of God! Jesus, the Bible, it's simply inaccurate historical records that evolved into mythology and was woven into our cultural being when people were less educated and didn't know as much as we now know today."

But that is actually the lie!

Think about what you have learned, from just a tiny little pocket book like this. You have learned how fundamentally flawed the big bang theory is and interspecies evolution. You have learned that archaeology, surprisingly, has provided a lot of real evidence to support the historical accuracy of the events recorded in the New Testament. You have come to appreciate that the New Testament is regarded as a historically accurate record of events even in the secular world. You have learned that there are more original manuscripts in existence today concerning the Bible than any other historical event of that time period. Furthermore, we have a situation where we have eye witnesses to these events who are named and appear of good character. There are no adverse witnesses arguing that the records were lies and we have no ulterior motives identified for what they recorded to be anything other than fact.

On top of all this we then have to explain how did all those prophecies get fulfilled if it was not divine in nature? How does one person fake the fulfilment of so many prophecies that were recorded 1,500 to 400 years before their birth? It doesn't make sense unless we at least **consider** there is some sort of divine involvement. What about the people? The billions of people throughout the last 2,000 years. Were they all duped? Were they all uneducated and easily fooled? If so then why is it still happening today across such a broad set of demographics when people are better educated?

In less than one hundred short pages we have probably dispelled at least a few myths that you would have taken as fact before you read this book. What more will you find when you dig deeper?

Believe me, I know, religion has been terribly twisted and manipulated by humankind. Terrible, terrible things have been done by bad people "in the name of God" and I will never defend or condone those things. However I learned, as I studied more, you don't have to defend the "church" or its actions to believe in God.

The Bible says, "where more than two of you meet in my name, there I am". The church is not some fancy building or ceremonial traditions. It's not decorated robes and a hierarchical system of bishops and deacons and the like. It's a simple gathering of people who believe in a living God.

I challenge you, **put aside all your prejudices**, sit down and still your mind, think through everything we have discussed and try to establish how things can be explained without there being some sort of God.

The reasoned person cannot find an explanation without some sort of divine being.

Better still, we were never asked to believe blindly. Evidence abounds. We were taught always to critically assess the scriptures so that we could develop a better intellectual understanding of God and his creation. God has provided us with his Word, to reveal to us the foolishness of following false gods. God who is free, has made us in his image, thereby also giving us free will. He has done this so that we might have the freedom to choose to be in a relationship with him, rather than to be compelled to be in a relationship with him.

This book stuck to facts. Hard facts that you can research yourself and that neither the secular or religious mainstream world contends. These include:

Jesus Christ was a real person, fact.

He was born around 5-6 BC and died around 30-36 AD, fact.

He provided religious teaching and did things that people couldn't explain, fact.

He was betrayed by one of his own disciples, handed over to Pontius Pilate and crucified, fact.

His followers believe he rose from the dead and following his death a great religious movement started that has continued to this day, fact.

None of the above statements are contended by anyone who is educated on the subject matter, believer or unbeliever. The only real point of contention is, "was Jesus who he said he was?"

The life raft is just over there, all you have to do is make the effort to swim up to it.

It's a big ocean though. The raft will still get tossed about, bad things will still happen, some people will fall off it and disappear, some people will be worried about if they will survive and some will give up. It certainly won't be all plain sailing. But it is real, and in the fullness of time it will get you to calmer waters.

My personal journey to faith spanned over a decade, it had many ups and downs and it is a journey I am still on to this day. However, I did eventually arrive at the point where I could no longer deny all the facts. The further you dive into researching the life of Jesus, the more apparent it becomes, that Jesus was a big sign post in the history of humankind pointing to God.

If this tiny book has in anyway prompted your interest, then please don't stop. The end of this book should really be just the beginning of a much longer journey for you.

First of all, consider going directly to the source and read one of the firsthand accounts of Jesus's life in the Gospels. The gospel of Mark is a great place to start. It's short, sharp and to the point.

Then consider reading other well researched literature written by credible authors. Timothy Keller, Rick Warren and Lee Strobel are three such authors who are all well respected and have many books for people seeking answers or who are starting out on their spiritual journey. There are countless other great authors, I only give you these names as their books have personally helped me on my own journey.

Finally, and most importantly, you will need people to talk to. Faith without fellowship doesn't work. You will need a teacher of some sort, to answer some of your questions and help you puzzle together the pieces for some of the more complex issues. You will need friends to help you out when things get tough. Try attending a few different churches in your area and experience it for yourself. You will know pretty quickly if one is right for you. If it is not, don't give up, try another one and continue trying until you find one with people that you can relate to. Once you find one then take the time and build some relationships. Ask questions and be prepared to really give it a go.

There is no magic formula, there is no one size fits all. Everyone is truly unique so you should expect that everyone's journey to God will be unique too. I just ask of you, please, don't get to the end of your life and say "I just never really thought about".

ABOUT THE AUTHOR

Giuliano Robert Sala Tenna was born in Perth, Western Australia the youngest of six siblings into a Roman Catholic family. Having lost his Mother to cancer at 12 years of age Giuliano lost his faith and wandered for over 15 years seeking meaning in the secular world.

Giuliano completed a Bachelor of Business degree at Curtin University of Technology with a double major in Economics and Finance, graduating with Distinctions, and proceeded to build a successful career in the Australian finance industry that has now spanned over 22 years.

Becoming a millionaire before the age of twenty seven and then almost losing everything during the global financial crisis, Giuliano has experienced the highs and lows this world has to offer.

Giuliano's journey back to faith was one built on reason and research, critical assessment and personal experiences, it is a journey that continues to this day.

Giuliano has been married for over 14 years to his beautiful wife, has two incredible sons, is a serving member of Claremont Baptist Church in Western Australia and remains active in the Australian finance industry being regularly quoted in the press and media.